SOUL SONGS

SOUL SONGS

EMILY SHEA

DAES Industries

Copyright © 2023 by Emily Shea

All rights reserved. No part of this book may be reproduced in any manner whatsoever without written permission except in the case of brief quotations embodied in critical articles and reviews.

The moral rights of the author have been asserted.

Instagram: e.s.words

Cover and internal illustrations purchased for use: https://creativemarket.com/anmark

First Printing, 2023

Contents

Dedication	x
mo anam cara	1
blossoming	2
love	3
her love	4
liminal	5
time	6
home	7
ocean's kiss	8
float	10
float in rain	12
rip	13
safe	14
sunrise	15
shine	16

waking	17
God painting	18
sunset reflections	19
same sky	20
anail ur	21
my love	22
stories	23
night gardens	24
communing love	26
fragrant love	27
my gift	28
soul friend	29
remember	30
loving me	31
pondering love	32
enveloping love	34
creation	36
first life	38
twin souls	39
communion	41
from dust to dust	42

samsara	43
holy ground	44
nitmiluk	45
light	46
Ancient One	47
grandmother	48
gentleness	49
twigs	50
breathnaigh	51
beatitude	52
wind	54
chased by rain	56
wet season	57
summer storms	58
sunset walks	59
loss	60
fragile	61
tapestry	62
knowing	63
ellipses	64
dance	65

memories	66
sound	67
tears	68
ocean's edge	69
on tears	70
despair	71
intimacy	72
gaze	73
reminder	74
compassion	75
contentment	76
secrets	78
grace	80
instead	81
the veil was torn	82
first friend	84
infinity	85
desert heart	86
Holy Spirit	87
spirit	88
About The Author	90

for my loves

mo anam cara

may our afters narrowly ache, may care always reach
athwart

blossoming

you are the spring buds
flowering after snowy carpets
melt into the dirt

love

gently
like a bud
opening
in the rain
open
your heart
to love
everyday

her love

have you had a friend
who loved you with words
more than physical touch
her heart
poured out
in symbols
simple
eloquent
soulful
she held you
in such a way
her heart burst
words spilling over pages
messing up your
existence

liminal

two souls
liminally meet
two people
gaze athwart
dinner forgotten
elemental stirring
long abandoned
physical hunger
anam cara
whispering souls
unite as
fingertips soft
initial touch
lips curious
kiss turned
starlit gardens
into home

time

when time stood still once
we shared a lifetime in a day
under the salty waves

home

immerse yourself
content
in salty water
it is home
wild but known
childhood dreams
of mermaid tails
adult memories
of family drawn close
waves that dump you into sand
waves that wash away your tears
rise chest first above them
float eyes closed aloft
wild abandon
trust
waves that feel like home

ocean's kiss

my ocean home
within your arms
foamy hands slipping
over clay stomach
ochre hair flowing
over naked breast
ocean skin meeting
sandy lipped sweetness

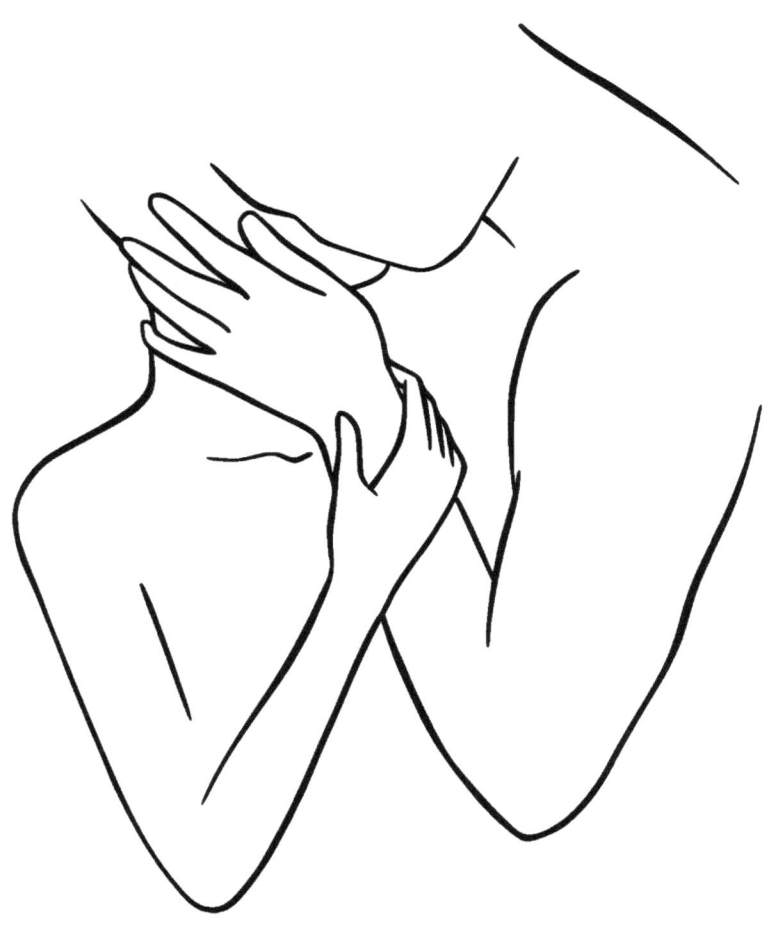

float

tidal waves

sweeping tendrils
of long brown hair
across freckled skin

body floating
in saltiness
allowing tension
to drift

ocean sounds
echoing in shell ears
perhaps a mermaid call
the whisper of a wish

she knows this
salty home
this bliss
hers alone

while ears sit
below surface
muted sounds
far off myths

reality is her
and salt
and this

float in rain

pattering rain
on saltwater
she floats
ears hidden
from earthly sounds
instead
water on water
pummels
patters
falls fresh
on closed eyelids
bouncing off
ocean skin
the sound of the wet
immersed in itself
and in her

rip

toes planted
in shifting sand
thighs straining
as current lures me
away from you
your voice fades
as firm and stoic you stand
I turn from you
diving under
foamy breakers
current hauling
my lithe body
fighting to be
shoreward bound

safe

solid rock
juts out of swirling waves
sand shifts at its base
feet sink
fingers grasp crevices
muscles strain
I pull higher
lift toes to cracks
calves contract
push upwards
body safe
atop the rock

sunrise

sun's soft rising hues
I wake soft dreaming of you
do you see it too

shine

the soft light
embraces the new day
with no expectation
but to shine

waking

grey sky
slipping into light
eyes flutter slow...
slowly
unlatching
you dawn
in my eyes
and in my heart

God painting

he paints the soft
watercolour blue
waiting for me to see
his brush hovers
grey-white clouds
puffing over azure
he sees me
I walk with him
feel his nudging
turn back
I turn and see
his masterpiece
in front of me

sunset reflections

One just has to look at the sun setting on a bad day to know that there is some insignificant part of me in this grand design that sets on one day and begins anew the next with light triumphing over dark.

And yet significance in calling and naming and imagery as creator resplendent in creation walks physically on earth in bodies of men and women as lights in a dark world.

And despite bad days walked in darkness the creator light within me looks with hopeful eyes at darkness obliterated by piercing light cutting like sword to bone as truth unfolds and hearts are made whole.

same sky

my sun is rising in cloudy skies
it is beautiful that the same sky
in all it's changing glory
sits above connecting us
though distant, the sun will always rise
and set, on days we share through love

anail ur

you are a fresh breath
on a grey and dreary day
carrying memory

my love

the soft
resting
of my head
on your shoulder
cloudy kisses
on my hair
arm circling
my waist
my heart
my home

stories

story-sharing punctuated by kisses
is a slower and more enjoyable way
to hear another's heart
connecting imagination & presence
in beautiful ways

night gardens

follow me
traipse along the
empty page

I will lead you
into night-time gardens
climbing curious walls

breaking proprietous
assumptions

if you wish
this starry night
lasts for all time

in memory
imagination
captured by us

in vine covered pathways
as we duck below branches

look upwards
and inwards

catch my hand
kiss me
before it ends

communing love

there is no perfect
just ones
who love you
despite your flaws
these ones
are uncommon
distinctive
loving you
individually
uniquely
completely
their essence
enveloping yours

fragrant love

possibilities of long love
becoming deep love
the strong and heady
fragrance of Love
weaving souls and skin
together again
transformational love
changing us
changing them
as fear is cast out
and life is renewed

my gift

you are a treasure
a precious gift
still surprising
your constancy
friendship and care
that we find
each other
after so many years

soul friend

most precious gift
of friendship given
truths spoken
stories heard
seen and known
grappled to my soul

remember

listening
the rise and fall
of your breathing
turning
my arm resting
across your chest
hearing
heart beats
gentle rhythms
remembering
times our hearts
beat together

loving me

loving me is easy
it takes little noticings
loving me is frangipanis
long luscious embraces
loving me is G&T in shadowy corners
running your fingers from my toes to my thighs
loving me is space and silence
allowing nights away for respite
loving me is laughter
any comedic bliss, especially the irish
loving me is lingerie and jewels
outback hikes and sand between my toes
loving me is salt water
peaches, strawberries, mangoes, dark chocolate
loving me is sustainable
lasting, or reusable, secondhand is fine
loving me is rocks and mountains
floating endlessly in oceans
really
loving me is easy

pondering love

does love exist
that has no requirements
no jealousy
or doubt
even God is jealous
desiring our love
firstly His
could I love you
without boundary
or prescription
no expectation
even of you
to love me back

or must love
hold expectation
for without
is it really love
if unmet
even disappointment
somehow reveals my love
that this is
not more fulfilling
you unchanged
yet I am here
loving you

enveloping love

there are rivers of love in me
flowing freely
if you would let them
they would envelop you

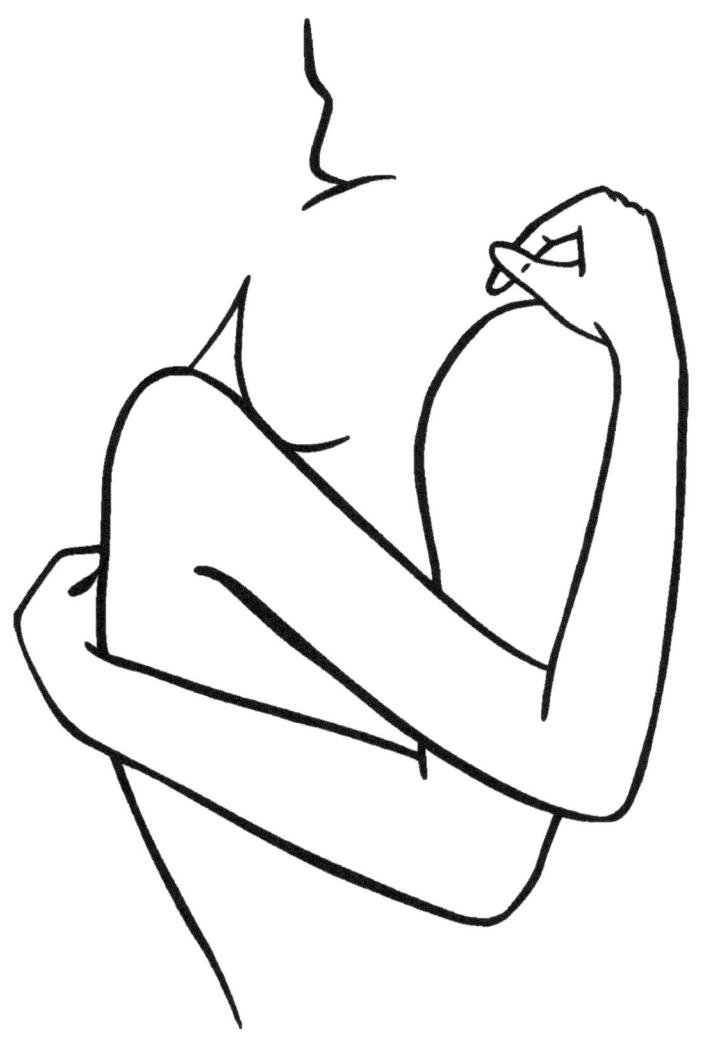

creation

hovering over water
still
quiet
listening
you leap
you laugh
you fly

kaleidoscope colours
life
light
growth
you breathe
you play
you paint

joyful abandon flows
peace
hope
love
you watch
you wait
you yearn

emptiness awaits you
dark
black
longing
you fill
you heal
you shine

first life

in clay lying
waiting
inchoate beings
gently extruded
held and warmed
moulded
shaped
breath suffusing
two vessels
held soul
born into being
bathed in light
separated
life lived
loved
shadowed a little
wandered
paths entwined
soul recognising
anam cara
softly
light shone again

twin souls

is it possible
two souls
never meet
despite
forming
together
in clay
could it be
another soul
entwines
and maybe
fulfils
but what if
twin souls
meet later
tugging stronger
unimaginable
sweetness
melody and harmony
echoing in memory
until drawn
together again

communion

and all the beauty
in the world
the wispy clouds
the soft sun
the verdant trees
pale in comparison to you,
the sweet communion
gifted shared received

from dust to dust

bare feet
let clay meet clay
soft footfalls
on red dirt
on sandy beach
grit underfoot
grinding death away
each step drawing
closer to understanding
from this
you came

samsara

trample me under your feet
that I might crumble
brown crisp specks
crushed into softness
mixing with dirt and decay
nourishing the next
generation

holy ground

stillness.
quiet.
beauty.
reverence.
awe.
whisper.
this is holy ground.

nitmiluk

sound ricocheted
off ancient rock
as burning skies
bathed red gorge in light
shadows rapidly fell
chasing birds into trees
turning sparkling water
to murky depths
crescent moon
slowly ascending
insect calls
sonorous in the still air
as silent human
leaves nature
to its
night

light

miniscule
fissure
piercing
stretching
expanding
brighter
luminous
dazzling
light

Ancient One

Golden orb of ancient light
Luminescent in the night
Darkness fading fast away
In the spaces where you stay

Music lilting over clouds
Wayward in its heavenly bounds
Starlight glimmers through the mist
Where once dark now lovers kiss

grandmother

ancient face lined deep
luminous eyes embracing
soul stories of grace

gentleness

- after David Tensen

What you can expect
is plenty of gentle nods
when you explain how life
crumbled under your feet
tossed you with the tides
changed you in every season
and gently woke you
with dawning light
to begin anew

twigs

small twigs
one by one
obstruct
harden my heart
water pressure
desiring to break
forces
cracks
ruptures
living water
flows through

breathnaigh

drench me in your gaze
cease time
heaviness
curious eyes
unsaid words
hang taut
in breathless spaces
dew collecting
meniscus bursting

sigh

silence broken
refreshing
my soul

beatitude

blessed are those who are disillusioned
for they will turn back to living hope

...

and as these words flow through my brain
your rain falls on the roof of my house

...

and they will find life

wind

eolian sound

reverberating

ears full of it

wondering how

moses felt

as God

moved by him

shutting my eyes

I walk on

bowing my head

noticing that this

eolian tune

quietens

wondering if this is why

we bow our heads

to pray

stopping the sound

in reverent thoughts

to listen

in between the buffering

to the

still small voice

of God

chased by rain

whispering breezes
gently caress
she dreams
time passes
temperature drops
as wilder
winds push
white walls
ever closer
islands vanish
ocean skin
accepting sky
water chasing
her inside

wet season

first clouds of the wet
rain plummeting as I wake
bright pink my first view

summer storms

intermittent
gentle drops
grace the petals
as the storm
rolls in

sunset walks

sunset ripples
humid winds
become
chill breeze
eolian voices
summoning rain
grey clouds
answer
heavy drops
soak me

loss

sometimes
it is in the between
the lost places
we find ourselves
wandering
winding pathways
of our minds
stemming from silence
from loss
amidst chaos
when we stop
memory awakes aching
hearts beckoning
across time
and space

fragile

can a soul crack
somehow mere mortality
seems more real today
like I will split open
blow on me
and pieces will fly in the wind
place your hand on my shoulder
it will crumble
though your touch is soft
speak love
I will weep

tapestry

if all the threads of the world were to unravel
would our threads somehow move closer
a tapestry falling to the ground
that lumpy soft mess on the floor
moving threads closer
never touching
suddenly threads would touch
unraveling further at the nearness of you
I am pared back
one loose strand
bare threads exposing vulnerability
your threads wrap around mine
strengthening again as our threads entwine

knowing

the profundity of it all
two souls
understanding
despite distance
strife and circumstance
the sweetness
of being known

ellipses

...
unsaid words sit here
in tiny dots
wonderings
unasked questions
soul-known thoughts
ponderings
in tiny dots
...

dance

music swells
I see you dance
tiny bright circles
behind shut eyes
forming you
in my mind
I am lost
in the music
and you

memories

i played you
in my head
a record spinning
hypnotic
words you spoke
memorised
to pull out
on rainy days
and study them
for truths
on joyous days
your smile dances
over melodies
on hard days
just the three
seen
understood
appreciated
these words
play back
to me

sound

saxophone on steroids
sound throbbed
through the car
tears wove
from corners
down her soft red cheek
to corners
salty on her tongue
holding memories
hopes and heartaches
as she drove home

tears

tears fall from tired eyes
as full heart shatters from full stops
and foolish times

ocean's edge

salt water meets
from eyes to feet

on tears

love appeared in my eyes
at first a tiny prick
water creeping slowly over rock
falling down it's smooth surface
rolling earthwards, filling crevices with hope

despair

if a tear
should creep
into your eyes
or despair
fill your heart
if thoughts
melancholy
plague you
or feelings
overwhelm
wrap your arms
around you
anam cara
I am there
my soul
pointing you
to light
when darkness
wants you
I will fight

intimacy

the tentative choice
to open her heart
and be seen
the explosion
of emotion
a geyser
rushing upwards
salt water
spurting from rock
bursting from
ocean eyes
she remembers
you held
more questions
unspoken
intimacy
found in
dark umber eyes

gaze

her smooth naked face
met compassion and kindness
in curious gaze

reminder

fatigued heart
mind
soul
just like
fatigued muscles
need a gentle reminder
they are still strong
warm them up
use them again
love fully
ponder
wonder
they too will remember
their strength

compassion

compassion carried
with it burdens
imagined thoughts
of your life
and what it lacked
or did not lack
i am not sure
the want to hold
when times are hard
to know the circle
of your heart
that you are loved
when despair
rears its ugly head
think of hope for me
know that you are seen
and hard hearts
have no place
with you
and me

contentment

I wrestled with the idea that somehow what I have is
not enough
that piece by little piece I need more
why when I know that contentment is the answer do I
look outside my box

is it just that I'm human that my mind is a mess of
wonderings and spaces best left shelved
is it that my human nature is flawed
that I cannot be truly content with my lot

the grass is greener where you water it
or where the summer rains fall
endlessly upon an overgrown garden
is there too much
too many weeds for one gardener to overcome

I have learned that life is an ebb and flow of thoughts
and time and space
that what I feel tonight tomorrow may have passed into
the abyss
and there I will be left with peace
contentment and love for what I have
and chaotic thoughts will have ceased

secrets

did you know
you carry my secrets
outside my mind
but I have never felt
your judgment
for my mistakes
only love

grace

life is not black and white
it is an ever-changing wash of greys
and grace
where unconditional love
hung on a tree
the sinner kneeled
as blood washed down
and grace let them live
ever redeeming
their every mistake
until such a time
they return to eternal bliss

instead

through your eyes
I am guilty no more
instead
overwhelming love
would shatter rocky outcrops
erupting from this heart
with each shifting of emotions
instead
overwhelming love
would dewy drops deliver
until cracked dirt
softened
opening to flourishing
instead
overwhelming love
would stand strong
hands outstretched
welcome and sacrifice
mingled
in eyes that pierced
mine

the veil was torn

it tore
the veil
some days
i try
to pull
it shut

i feel
my shame
my guilt
fabric between
clenched fists

your gentle
playful tug
softens heart
reminding me

you love
through
broken body
shed blood
torn veil
faithful promise

eden like
intimacy flows
letting go
of veil

first friend

closer
than another
first friend
in my heart
your triune presence
enveloping me
in love

infinity

hold me
in infinite arms
so spacious
and yet
snug
bespoke
I alone
am made to be
and yet
you hold infinity

desert heart

She threw a last shoot through her cracked heart
'Sky do you see me?' She called to the vast expanse
Just as she thought it would wither and her
desert heart crumble
The sky dripped.
Slow steady drops.
Slow soaking drops.
The water filled each gap, soaking, joining,
allowing roots to grow
Her final shoot steady and secure in life-giving soil

Holy Spirit

your all consuming
encapsulating
surrounding
deepening presence
draws my heart
my eyes
my soul and mind
in passionate desire
to know you

spirit

soft
caresses
surround me
your presence
gently touching
even to the depths
of my aching soul

Emily is a Jesus follower, a wife, a mother to four boys, an educator, a musician, a curious and thoughtful soul.

She has written songs from her teenage years and poetry from time to time.

More recently, her poetic work has flowed out of life, relationships and all the complexities of loving and being loved.

These poems also find home in her love for nature, hiking, climbing, and the healing gift of swimming in the ocean.

www.ingramcontent.com/pod-product-compliance
Lightning Source LLC
Chambersburg PA
CBHW040243010526
44107CB00065B/2854